Sunday
Sunday
Sunda
nday Sun
Sunday

Presented to

_____

On the occasion of

_____

From

_____

Date

_____

Sunday

Compiled by
Helen Hosier

BARBOUR
PUBLISHING, INC.

Published by Barbour Publishing, Inc., P.O. Box 719, Uhrichsville, Ohio 44683
http://www.barbourbooks.com

 Member of the
Evangelical Christian
Publishers Association

Printed in China.

Sunday

The Sabbath and Sunday…

ORIGINS

Safely Through Another Week
John Newton (1725-1807), Lowell Mason (1792-1872)

Safely through another week
God has brought us on our way;
Let us now a blessing seek,
Waiting in His courts today:
Day of all the week the best,
Emblem of eternal rest. . . .
Here we come Thy name to praise
Let us feel Thy presence near;
May Thy glory meet our eyes
While we in Thy house appear;
Here afford us, Lord, a taste
Of our everlasting feast. . . .
May Thy gospel's joyful sound
Conquer sinners, comfort saints;
May the fruits of grace abound,
Bring relief for all complaints:
Thus may all our Sabbaths prove,
Till we join the Church above.

Keeping Sunday Special

Remember the Sabbath day by keeping it holy. Six days you shall labor and do all your work, but the seventh day is a Sabbath to the LORD your God. On it you shall not do any work, neither you, nor your son or daughter, nor your manservant or maidservant, nor your animals, nor the alien within your gates. For in six days the LORD made the heavens and the earth, the sea, and all that is in them, but he rested on the seventh day. Therefore the LORD blessed the Sabbath day and made it holy," Exodus 20:8–11, NIV.

While the Sabbath, which was a Saturday and the seventh day, was given specifically to Israel, the church from the very beginning met on the first day of the week because that's when Jesus rose from the dead. That's when the church was born; the day of Pentecost was on the day after the Sabbath. Matthew Henry explains that "the law was given by Moses, but grace and truth came by Jesus Christ." Dr. J. Vernon McGee wrote: "The church is a new creation and it was given a new day to observe which is the first day of the week."

Thus it is that we, like the Israelites to whom the law was given, still honor God when we seek to keep Sunday special.

God's Gift

"Bear in mind
that the LORD has given you the Sabbath;
that is why on the sixth day
he gives you bread for two days."
Moses speaking in Exodus 16:29, NIV

$\mathcal{T}$he first thing the Lord made known to the whole community of Israelites concerning this day, this one different day a week, was that it was a gift! Because God wanted the people to have a rest, He made it possible to have one day a week. One-seventh of time is to be a day to look back at the amazing reality of God's having worked to create the earth in six days, and then having rested the seventh. He, the Creator, who we are told never is tired or weary, rested from creating all that He created.

What does that mean? It means a tremendously important thing. Just because we cannot dissect and analyze all that God means when He tells us He rested, or when He tells us He has hallowed this day and blessed it to be a special day, does not mean we are to toss it out as a concept we can't get to the bottom of.

The Creator is speaking to all human beings; He has made it the fourth commandment in the first four relating to our duties to God. We are to respect this day; He has commanded us to respect it. Our Heavenly Father has made it emphatically definite that this proportion of time set aside to be different in some practical way is to be a sign, an outward sign of an inward reality, that we are His people.

EDITH SCHAEFFER
IN *LIFELINES: THE TEN
COMMANDS FOR TODAY*

"...that this proportion of time set aside to be different in some practical way is to be a sign, an outward sign of an inward reality, that we are His people."

Commandment to Obey?

*T*here is a story told in Benjamin Franklin's autobiography of a clergyman who was ordered to read the proclamation issued by Charles I, bidding the people to return to sports on Sundays. To his congregation's horror and amazement, he did read the royal edict in church, which many clergy had refused to do. But he followed it with the words, "Remember the Sabbath day to keep it holy," and added: "Brethren, I have laid before you the commandment of your king and the Commandment of your God. I leave it to you to judge which of the two ought rather to be observed."

CHRISTIAN HERALD

Our great-grandfathers called it the holy Sabbath;
our grandfathers, the Sabbath;
our fathers, Sunday;
but today we call it the weekend.
WESLEYAN METHODIST

This Day at Thy Creating Word

William Walsham How, 1823–1897

This day at Thy creating Word
First o'er the earth the light was poured:
O Lord, this day upon us shine
And fill our souls with light divine.

This day the Lord for sinners slain
In might victorious rose again:
O Jesus, may we raiséd be
From death of sin to life in Thee!

This day the Holy Spirit came
With fiery tongues of cloven flame:
O Spirit, fill our hearts this day
With grace to hear and grace to pray.

O day of light and life and grace,
From earthly toil sweet resting place,
Thy hallowed hours, blest gift of love,
Give we again to God above.

The Sabbath (Sunday)
A REMINDER OF REST

Jesus' Inaugural Address for His Ministry

The scene: Jesus in the Synagogue at Nazareth, the place where He grew up.

His friends and relatives and neighbors gathered in great excitement. They had watched Him grow to manhood; they knew His parents, Mary and Joseph. So they were astonished at His air of authority as He strode to the center of the crowded stone room and was handed the book of the prophet Isaiah from the Torah shrine. He found the passage He wanted, then read the ancient prophecy: "The Spirit of the Lord is on me, because he has anointed me to preach good news to the poor. He has sent me to proclaim freedom for the prisoners and recovery of sight for the blind, to release the oppressed, to proclaim the year of the Lord's favor," Isaiah 61:1–2.

Jesus handed the Scriptures back to the attendant and stared quietly at the rows of townspeople. "Today," He said slowly, "this Scripture is fulfilled in your hearing."

At first there were gasps, then excited murmurings. Then one of the elders called out sarcastically, "Isn't this Joseph's son?"

Others laughed. After all, this young man was merely a hometown boy, a carpenter and the son of a carpenter. Jesus knew what they were thinking. "No prophet is accepted in his hometown."

This humble message at the remote Nazareth synagogue was the inaugural address for Jesus' entire ministry. Through it He formally announced His messiahship and the rule of God in this world. As a result, human history was forever altered.

The Kingdom of God had come.

THE GOSPEL OF LUKE 4:18–30
AS TOLD BY CHARLES COLSON IN *KINGDOMS IN CONFLICT*

"On the First Day of the Week..."

The Resurrection of the Living Lord

𝒯he Resurrection is the star in the firmament of Christianity. "On the first day of the week Mary Magdalene went to the tomb early, and saw that the stone had been taken away from the tomb. Mary stood outside by the tomb weeping. Jesus said to her, 'Mary! . . . go to My brethren.' Mary came and told the disciples that she had seen the Lord, and that He had spoken these things to her."

Surprised by joy, Mary could hardly wait to share the great "good news." "Then, the same day at evening, being the first day of the week, when the doors were shut where the disciples were assembled, for fear of the Jews, Jesus came and stood in the midst, and said to them, 'Peace be with you.' Then Jesus said to them again, 'Peace to you! As the Father has sent Me, I also send you.' And when He had said this, He breathed on them, and said to them, 'Receive the Holy Spirit.' " (selected portions from John 20, NKJV).

Jesus stood "in their midst," beyond the agony, beyond the

tragedy, beyond the darkness that had so filled their hearts with terror. His first words to them were words of peace—words meant to calm and soothe their minds and wondering hearts. Jesus supplied tangible evidence—the marks of the wounds remained on His body after the Resurrection—that they might be demonstrations of the truth of it. Jesus immediately brought the disciples back to the place where there was a recognition of responsibility. He entrusted them with a tremendous commission. To qualify them for their great mission, He gave them the gift of the Holy Spirit. Resources would be at their disposal that they had never had before, and they would be equal to the work set before them in that power.

"And when He had said this, He breathed on them, and said to them, 'Receive the Holy Spirit.'"

In the same way it is He Who is our strong consolation; the peace was won for us also through His suffering, and to us also has access to that power been given.

HELEN KOOIMAN HOSIER
IN *JESUS: LOVE IN ACTION*

Jesus' Understanding of Holiness

*B*oth Jesus and the Pharisees agreed that being holy was of fundamental importance. They agreed that God's historical purpose was to call out a people for Himself; that this people would be a holy people and that their holiness, or difference, would be seen in their behavior and outlook. Jesus demonstrated in His Sermon on the Mount how clearly He believed that we were to be different. In Matthew 6:8 He said, "Do not be like them" (NIV). Our character is to be completely distinct from what the world celebrates.

Jesus took holiness seriously, but the Pharisees moaned over Jesus' abuse of the Sabbath. Why wouldn't He heal Monday–Wednesday–Friday? Even a Tuesday–Thursday routine would have been fine. Why did He have to pick the Sabbath? They felt His healing on the Sabbath constituted work. Jesus said their interpretation was wrong: "The Sabbath was made for man, not man for the Sabbath" (Mark 2:27, NIV). Jesus was not saying that rest on the Sabbath was unimportant. But the Pharisees said they wanted to live according to God's laws; so, ironically, while they carefully avoided working on the Sabbath, they plotted to kill Jesus.

REBECCA MANLEY PIPPERT
IN *OUT OF THE SALTSHAKER*

With Joy We Hail the Sacred Day

Harriet Auber, 1773–1862

With joy we hail the sacred day
Which God has called His own;
With joy the summons we obey
To worship at His throne.

Spirit of grace, O deign to dwell
Within Thy church below!
Make her in holiness excel,
With pure devotion glow.

Let peace within her walls be found;
Let all her sons unite;
To spread with grateful zeal around
Her clear and shining light.

The "Fatherland"

This visible world we now live in is, to us, what the desert was for the people of Israel. Those people of old wandered in vain as they looked for their "fatherland"—but those times when they let the Father Himself be their Guide, they made progress and did not lose their way. God's "way" for those people was obedience to His commandments. Because they overlooked or ignored the spiritual path, they never attained the land where they would have found the blessing and the rest they wanted.

So often, we allow ourselves to be sidetracked from following Him because we focus our attention on temporal affairs. We let the world tempt us with what is "good" according to its evil standards, and even as believers we forget that we are on a spiritual pilgrimage.

If you don't want to die of thirst in the desert of this world, let your soul drink of God's love. This is the fountain God has chosen to place in this world, to keep us from fainting on our way home to Him.

AUGUSTINE FROM *HOMILIES ON THE FIRST EPISTLE OF JOHN:1*

*Without a Sabbath,
no worship;
without worship,
no religion;
and without religion,
no permanent
freedom.*
MONTALEMBERT

O what a blessing is Sunday,
interposed between the waves of worldly business
like the divine path of the Israelites through the sea!
There is nothing in which I would advise you
to be more strictly conscientious than
in keeping the Sabbath day holy.
I can truly declare that to me
the Sabbath has been invaluable.
WILBERFORCE

Blessed Day of Rest and Cheer

Joel Blomqvist, 1840–1930
Translated by Andrew L. Skoog, 1856–1934

Blessed day of rest and cheer!
Day divine, to us so dear!
When we gather, old and young,
Joining here in pray'r and song.

Now the week of toil is o'er,
And in peace we sit once more
In Thy presence, gracious Lord,
Waiting for Thy holy Word.

Lord, our God, we seek Thy face,
Bless us with sustaining grace;
May Thy heralds ev'rywhere,
Faithfully Thy truth declare.

Let Thy mighty word hold sway,
Over all our hearts today;
Hung'ring souls, good Shepherd, feed,
Into pastures green us lead.

May, O Lord, the day be near,
When we pass from trials here
Into Thine eternal rest,
In the mansions of the blest.

*The Sabbath is God's special present
to the workingman, and one of its chief objects
is to prolong his life, and preserve efficient
his working tone. The savings bank of human
existence is the weekly Sabbath.*
BLAIKIE

> *The longer I live the more highly do I estimate the Christian Sabbath, and the more grateful do I feel to those who impress its importance on the community.*
>
> DANIEL WEBSTER

Jesus in the Temple

When Jesus was twelve years old, he accompanied his parents to Jerusalem for the annual Passover Festival, which they attended each year. After the celebration was over, they started home to Nazareth, but Jesus stayed behind in Jerusalem. His parents didn't miss Him the first day. But when He didn't show up that evening, they started to look for Him.

Three days later, they finally discovered Him. He was in the Temple, sitting among the teachers of law, discussing deep questions with them and amazing everyone with His understanding and answers.

His parents didn't know what to think. "Why did you need to search?" he asked. "Didn't you realize that I would be here at the Temple, in my Father's house?" (Excerpts from Luke 2:41–49, TLB).

"Didn't you realize that I would be here at the Temple, in my Father's house?"

These first recorded words of Jesus are an index and an explanation of His entire career, a revelation of the consciousness of Divine Sonship. Jesus already realized that, in a unique sense, God was His own Father, the true source of His being. Most important of all, these words are the revelation of a firm resolve; Jesus perceived that it was His duty to be in the house of His Father—not merely in the literal Temple, but in the sphere of life and activity of which the Temple was the great expression and symbol and sign. He had determined to devote all His thoughts and energies and powers to the definite service of God. [Are we not also] to recognize in the service of God the supreme and comprehensive duty of every life?

EXCERPTED FROM *THE GOSPEL OF LUKE*, COMMENTARY BY CHARLES R. ERDMAN

The Church
SUNDAY'S COMPANION

What Is the Church?

The church is many things. It is weddings and holy vows spoken in love and reverence. It is funerals and the promise of life eternal. It is babies being baptized. It is comfort and hope for a better tomorrow. It is Easter lilies. It is worn hymnbooks. It is work and sacrifice and Holy Communion.

The church is little children singing, "Jesus Loves Me." It is robed choirs singing anthems of praise. It is Christmas carols and little boys in bathrobes being wise men and shepherds, little girls in nightgowns portraying angels.

The church is stained glass windows. It is an altar, a pulpit, and God's Word in a big leather book. It is fellowship dinners and foreign missions. It is a helping hand. It is a sermon that lifts the spirit. It is the sound of chairs scraping the floor in the Sunday school rooms. It is a bell ringing clear on a crisp, still morning. It is an organ's deep tones. It is heads bowed in prayer, a warm, friendly handclasp, a solemn whispered benediction. The church is giving and receiving. It is budgets and figures. It is wood and bricks and stone. It is goodness and mercy. It is a manger bed, a star, and a cross. It is a way of life.

CHARLES O. AUSTIN, JR.

$\mathcal{A}$ world without a Sabbath
would be like a man without a smile,
like a summer without flowers,
and like a homestead without a garden.
It is the joyous day of the whole week.
H. W. BEECHER

Sunday
is the core
of our civilization,
dedicated
to thought
and reverence.
EMERSON

Never Say, "I'm Just a Sunday School Teacher."

Written by Henrietta Mears, a Christian Educator ahead of her time. She was the inspirational genius of the great Sunday school of the First Presbyterian Church of Hollywood, California, and demonstrated to the world that Sunday school is important business and can be successful. Her great mind, prolific pen, and contagious enthusiasm made her one of the greatest influences of this century in furthering the work of the Sunday school across North America.

*D*on't ever say, "I'm *just* a Sunday school teacher." If you were a professor at Harvard or Oxford, you would be proud of it— proud of the great responsibility. Teacher, you are a professor in Christ's college. As a Sunday school teacher, you can be equally proud—not the sort of pride that exalts itself, but the warm joyful glow of humble satisfaction that comes to those who serve the Savior in His strength, not theirs.

What a responsibility you have—to teach an immortal soul to

have fellowship with God! To fulfill this responsibility you must be wholly dedicated to the Lord and to the task He has for you to do. Christ was a Teacher. He told you and me that our commission is to teach (Matthew 28:19–20). Don't ever say, "I'm *just* a Sunday school teacher." You are a teacher in Christ's college. Know your subject matter. Be proud that you teach!

> *You are a teacher in Christ's college. Know your subject matter. Be proud that you teach!*

Sunday Results

The holiest moment of the Sunday church service is the moment when God's people–strengthened by preaching and Sacrament–go out of the church door into the world to be the Church. We don't go to church; we are the Church.

ERNEST SOUTHCOTT

Origin of the Sunday School

> *A child in our Sunday schools knows more about God than all you can find in all the analects of Confucius.*
>
> CHARLES OGILVIE

The Sunday school was not originated by famous theologians. In 1780, businessman Robert Raikes saw dirty children on Sunday afternoon with their favorite activity: fist fights. Sunday afternoon was the only free day from hard work then.

Mr. Raikes established the first Sunday school with these children. It was promptly dubbed "Raikes Regiment" and "Billy Wild Goose." For those who came, he gave pennies; teachers were hired at twenty-five cents per Sunday. Later, John Wesley was the first to suggest the elimination of payment, and the movement spread.

Chased Out of Churches

*T*he first Sunday schools were chased out of churches. The Boston Park Street Church recorded in 1817, their fears that it might be a desecration of the Sabbath, and that children ought to be instructed by their parents in the home. Furthermore, it was felt that professing Christians ought to be at home engaging in reading, meditation, and prayer, instead of going outside their homes to teach children of other families on the Sabbath. But that church finally did start a Sunday school.

Founding of the American Sunday School Union

One of the oldest Christian organizations in the United States, and one that has veered little from its original purpose, is the American Sunday School Union founded in a schoolroom at Fourth and Vine Streets, in Philadelphia on May 13, 1817. Francis Scott Key, author of "The Star-Spangled Banner," helped to get it off the ground. Within ten years it had become the foremost publisher of children's literature. In its first century, more than 100,000 Sunday schools were established.

CHRISTIANITY TODAY

America's First Church

When I first went to Virginia, I well remember, we did hang an awning (which is an old sail) to three or four trees to shadow us from the sun. Our walls were rails of wood, our seats unhewed trees till we cut planks; our pulpit a bar of wood nailed to two neighboring trees; in foul weather we shifted into an old rotten tent, for we had few better, and this came by the way of adventure for new.

This was our church till we built a homely thing like a barn, set upon cratchets, covered with rafts, sedge, and earth; so was also the walls; the best of our houses of the like curiosity, but the most part far much worse workmanship, that could neither well defend wind nor rain, yet we had daily common prayer morning and evening, every Sunday two sermons, and every three months the Holy Communion till our minister died. But our prayers daily, with an homily on Sundays, we continued two or three years after, till more preachers came. Moreover, every man was required to attend, or pay a fine of so many pounds of tobacco—which was the currency of that day.

Captain John Smith, 1580–1631

The Church of God Is One

Daniel W. Whittle, 1840–1901

The church of God is one:
As brethren here we meet;
For us salvation's work is done,
In Christ we stand complete.

The church of God is one:
One only Lord we know;
We worship Jesus, God's own Son,
Who came God's love to show.

The church of God is one;
All, sinners saved by grace;
Our plea, the precious Blood alone;
The cross, our meeting place.

The church of God is one, Is one in faith and love,
Is one in the death by Jesus borne, one in His life above.

The Church:
The Custodian of the Gospel

All the blessings of peace and tranquility, without which there can be no stable social order and no civilization as we know it, are the result of the gospel. And the true Church is the custodian of that gospel. Therefore, the true Church is not only the central and fundamental, but also the vital institution upon which every other structure—social, political, and governmental—depends. Without the moral and spiritual light shed abroad by the Word of God through the Church, there would be no favorable climate for business and commerce or enlightening cultural, educational, and social activities. What we know as Western civilization, providing the highest standard of living, the greatest freedom and personal security, the most domestic peace and tranquility the world has ever known, is definitely a by-product of the Judeo-Christian ethic and the Redemption wrought by Jesus Christ.

Jesus was not speaking in fables when He said to His disciples in Matthew 5:13–14: "Ye are the salt of the earth. . . . Ye are the light of the world." The world at large is totally blind to this fact, but if it were not for the purifying and preserving influence of the

Church, the fabric of all we call civilization would totally disintegrate, decay, and disappear. The Church, in union with her risen and enthroned Lord is, therefore, the fundamental preserving factor in this present world order.

If it were not for the Church, Satan would already have turned this earth into hell.

PAUL E. BILLHEIMER
IN *DESTINED FOR THE THRONE*

*"Ye are the salt of the earth.
. . .Ye are the light of the world."*
MATTHEW 5:13–14

To the Little Girl
Who Sits in Front of Me in Church

How many Sundays
I have smiled to see
Your small gold head
three rows in front of me,
And how your soft smooth hair
curved out to seek
The most engaging dimple in your cheek.
How many times,
the service incomplete,
Grown tired, you've turned
and knelt upon the seat
And stared across the back of it at me
With childhood's
 infinite solemnity!
Do you recall the day,
convention scorning,
I said to you, with silent lips,
 "Good morning."

And how your wide,
unsmiling gaze grew more
Inscrutable
than it had been before!
Alas, that guardian angels
should elect
To make so small a maid
so circumspect!
For two whole Sundays
I have hoped in vain
You would relent
and turn around again.
And then, today,
oh, grave enchanting child,
How suddenly and dazzlingly
you smiled!

SARA HENDERSON HAY

Why Is the Church Significant to the World?

Why is the church significant to the world? Because the church represents penetrating light and undiluted salt in a lost, confused, insipid society. Interestingly, when a church remains neutral on a moral issue that affects the community, the public will criticize that church. The public will state that it has let the community down. In the public arena, the Church of Jesus Christ is expected to stand for righteousness. Even the uncommitted, the nonchurch crowd know in their hearts that a church that is weak regarding sin has lost its way.

When the pulpit denounces sin, people are influenced to stand against it. When the pulpit speaks on moral issues, people learn to penetrate the fog of compromise and gain courage to stand alone. For many, many years in our nation the church gave our nation its conscience. As its pulpits stood, its people stood.

"You are the salt of the earth," said Jesus. "You are the light on a hill. Don't put a bushel basket over it." Let the light shine. Let the salt bite. That's your role, Christian! The world expects it from us, even though it doesn't agree. In Paul's day "the whole praetorian guard" became aware of Christ! [See Philippians 1:12–14.] Even though many will not enter the doors of a local church (though they are invited), they expect us to stand for the truth as we see it in the Scripture. To do less is to diminish our distinctive and to lose our integrity.

CHARLES R. SWINDOLL
IN *GROWING DEEP IN THE CHRISTIAN LIFE*

When You Go to Church...

Enemy-occupied territory–that is what this world is. Christianity is the story of how the rightful king has landed, you might say landed in disguise, and is calling us all to take part in a great campaign of sabotage. When you go to church you are really listening in to the secret wireless from our friends: That is why the enemy is so anxious to prevent us from going.

C. S. LEWIS
IN *MERE CHRISTIANITY*

The Church Affecting the World

*T*he Church, if it is to affect the world, must become a center from which new spiritual power emanates. While the Church must be secular in the sense that it operates in the world, if it is only secular it will not have the desired effect upon the secular order which it is called to penetrate. With no diminution of concern for people, we can and must give new attention to the production of a trustworthy religious experience.

No man is strong enough or devout enough to operate alone. Even solitary worship is much more productive if it is enriched by the remembered experience of gathered worship. Iron sharpens iron (Proverbs 27:17). It is literally true, in the best experiences of joint worship, that the whole is greater than the sum of the parts. Though there may be religions in which solitariness is the highest expression of devotion, this is never true for the Christian, who understands that, bad as the Church may be, life without it is worse. The point is not that men cannot worship alone, but rather that they are more likely to be invigorated and sent out into the world as new persons if they are participants in the joint experience of a loving and reverent company of their fellow seekers.

ELTON TRUEBLOOD
IN *THE NEW MAN FOR OUR TIME*

A Home for Your Heart

Heaven knows no difference between Sunday morning and Wednesday afternoon. God longs to speak as clearly in the workplace as He does in the sanctuary. He longs to be worshiped when we sit at the dinner table and not just when we come to His communion table. You may go days without thinking of Him, but there's never a moment when He's not thinking of you. Wherever you are, whatever time it is, you are only a decision away from the presence of your Father.

MAX LUCADO
IN *THE GREAT HOUSE OF GOD*

New Testament Christianity, the Early Church, and Contemporary Christians

*T*he early Church lived dangerously. There was what J. B. Phillips calls "a suprahuman power" working through and energizing them and exerting a widespread influence. There was an excitement that was contagious; an unconquerable fellowship, an active, energetic Spirit of truth present, with the courage to match their new vision. Whatever "it" was, "it" worked, moving in on the human scene with astonishing impact.

G. K. Chesterton has made the observation that whatever else man is, he is not what he was meant to be. The question is in order: Why?

J. B. Phillips offers this explanation: "I am convinced that there will be no recovery of the vitality and vigor of New Testament Christianity until we who call ourselves

Christians dare to break through contemporary habits of thought and touch the resources of God" (excerpted from *New Testament Christianity*).

In John's Gospel, Jesus warned his disciples of the enmity they could expect from the world, and then he added an important "but." "But I will send you the Comforter–the Holy Spirit, the source of all truth" (John 15:26).

Here is the resource J. B. Phillips (and others) are referring to when they speak of the need for the God-given vigor that the early Church experienced.

HELEN KOOIMAN HOSIER
IN *JESUS: LOVE IN ACTION*

If the Sunday had not been observed as a day of rest during the last three centuries, I have not the slightest doubt that we should have been at this moment a poorer people and less civilized.
·MACAULAY

The Vital Place of the Church

The highest expression of the will of God in this age is the Church which He purchased with His own blood. According to the Scriptures the Church is the habitation of God through the Spirit. . . The Church is found wherever the Holy Spirit has drawn together a few persons who trust Christ for their salvation, worship God in spirit and have no dealings with the world and the flesh. The members may by necessity be scattered over the surface of the earth and separated by distance and circumstances, but in every true member of the Church is the homing instinct and the longing of the sheep for the fold and the Shepherd. Give a few real Christians half a chance and they will get together and organize and plan regular meetings for prayer and worship. In these meetings they will hear the Scriptures expounded, break bread together in one form or another according to their light, and try as far as possible to spread the saving gospel to the lost world.

"The gates of hell shall not prevail against her."

A. W. TOZER

Such groups are cells in the Body of Christ, and each one is a true church, a real part of the greater Church. It is in and through these cells that the Spirit does His work on earth. Whoever scorns the local church scorns the Body of Christ.

The Church is still to be reckoned with.

COMPILED BY
WARREN W. WIERSBE,
THE BEST OF A. W. TOZER

How Beautiful the Sight
James Montgomery, 1771–1854

How beautiful the sight
    Of brethren
        who agree
    In friendship
        to unite,
And bonds of charity;

For there
    the Lord commands
        Blessings,
    a boundless store,
From His unsparing hands,
Yea, life forevermore;
    Thrice happy they
        who meet above
    To spend eternity
        in love!

We Gather Together

Netherlands Folk hymn; translated by Theodore Baker

"God be merciful to us and bless us,
And cause His face to shine upon us."
Psalm 67:1, *NKJV*

We gather together to ask the Lord's blessing;
He chastens and hastens His will to make known;
The wicked oppressing now cease from distressing,
Sing praises to His name: He forgets not His own.
Beside us to guide us, our God with us joining,
Ordaining, maintaining His kingdom divine;
So from the beginning the fight we are winning;
Thou, Lord, wast at our side, all glory be Thine!
We all do extol Thee, Thou Leader triumphant,
And pray that Thou still our Defender wilt be.
Let Thy congregation escape tribulation:
Thy name be ever praised! O Lord, make us free!

The First Church of Jerusalem

*N*ext in importance to the coming of the Lord Jesus Christ to this earth, is the coming of the Holy Spirit. The Church was born on that day of Pentecost. Become familiar with this account, given in Acts 2:1–13.

What a Church was this First Church of Jerusalem, organized with a membership of 3,000 on the day of Pentecost! What glorious days followed, in "teaching" and "fellowship," and "signs and wonders," and, above all, salvation! The Lord added to the church daily such as should be saved (Acts 2:47). This is the real objective of the Church. Are we seeing it today in our churches?

HENRIETTA MEARS
IN *WHAT THE BIBLE IS ALL ABOUT*

*W*hen the day of Pentecost came, they were all together
in one place. Suddenly a sound like the blowing
of a violent wind came from heaven
and filled the whole house where they were sitting.
ACTS 2:1–3, NIV

"Jesus Christ Is Precious"

At one time in his life John Newton was a wreck of a man if ever there was one. He was a hard, rough, dirty sailor with a foul mouth and an appetite for rotten living. He hated life and life hated him.

Someone placed in the hands of this derelict a copy of Thomas á Kempis's *The Imitation of Christ*. Then a fearful experience in a storm at sea, together with his recovery from a dreaded illness in Africa, brought Newton to the point of view where he began to wonder about God. On his last voyage out as the captain of a slaveship, he met a man who helped bring him to faith in Christ. From then on, the point of view of John Newton changed. He began to love life and life loved him. And he went all about England sharing his faith.

> 'Twas grace that taught my heart to fear, and grace my fears relieved.
>
> JOHN NEWTON

When he was well past the "retirement age," he had to have an assistant stand in the pulpit with him on Sundays to help him with his sermons. Nothing could keep this man from preaching while he still had breath. One Sunday while delivering his message he repeated the sentence, "Jesus Christ is precious."

His helper whispered, "You've already said that twice."

"Yes," the elderly Newton replied, "and I'm going to say it again." The stones in the sanctuary fairly shook as the grand old preacher said again, "Jesus Christ is precious!"

Many today remember him as the author of several notable hymns, but John Newton never forgot who he was: a former libertine, a former slave captain, a former lost, lonely, and unloved seaman—but one who had learned that Jesus Christ is precious.

Poor, weak, and worthless though I am
I have a rich, almighty Friend;
Jesus, the Savior, is His Name;
He freely loves, and without end.
JOHN NEWTON

Amazing Grace

One of the most-loved hymns of all time,
composed by John Newton

Amazing grace, how sweet the sound
That saved a wretch like me!
I once was lost but now am found,
Was blind but now I see.
'Twas grace that taught my heart to fear,
And grace my fears relieved;
How precious did that grace appear,
The hour I first believed!

Thru many dangers, toils and snares,
I have already come;
'Tis grace hath brought me safe thus far,
And grace will lead me home.
When we've been there ten thousand years,
Bright shining as the sun,
We've no less days to sing God's praise,
Than when we'd first begun.

Sanctuary

To all who are weary and seek rest,
To all who mourn and long for comfort,
To all who struggle and desire victory,
To all who sin and need a Savior,
To all who are idle and look for service,
To all who are strangers and want fellowship,
To all who hunger and thirst after righteousness—
The church opens wide her doors and offers her
welcome in the name of
Jesus Christ her Lord.

AUTHOR UNKNOWN

*The test of a preacher is that his congregation
goes away saying, not "What a lovely sermon,"
but "I will do something."*
ST. FRANCIS DE SALES, 1562–1622

Morbus Sabbaticus, or Sunday Sickness

Morbus Sabbaticus, or Sunday sickness, is a disease peculiar to church members.

- The symptoms vary, but it never interferes with the appetite.
- It never lasts more than twenty-four hours.
- No physician is ever called.
- It always proves fatal in the end—to the soul!
- It is becoming fearfully prevalent, and is destroying thousands every year.

The attack comes on suddenly every Sunday. No symptoms are felt on Saturday night; the patient sleeps well and wakes feeling well and eats a hearty breakfast. But about church time the attack comes on and continues until services are over for the morning. Then the patient feels easy and eats a hearty dinner. In the afternoon he feels much better, and is able to take a walk and read the Sunday papers; and afterwards eats a hearty supper. But about church time he has another attack and stays at home. He wakes up Monday morning refreshed and able to go to work.

SOURCE UNKNOWN

*Let us not neglect
our church meetings. . .
but encourage
and warn each other,
especially now
that the day
of his coming back
again is drawing near.*
Hebrews 10:25, TLB

*Sundays observe; think when the bells to chime,
'Tis angels' music.*
GEORGE HERBERT (1593–1632)

The Church's One Foundation

Samuel J. Stone, Samuel S. Wesley

The Church's one foundation
Is Jesus Christ her Lord,
She is His new creation
By water and the word;
From heaven He came and sought her
To be His holy bride;
With His own blood He bought her,
And for her life He died.

Elect from ev'ry nation,
Yet one o'er all the earth,
Her charter of salvation,
One Lord, one faith, one birth;
One holy name she blesses,
Partakes one holy food,
And to one hope she presses,
With ev'ry grace endued. Amen.

An Hour
in Thy Presence

Lord, what a change within us one short hour
Spent in Thy presence will prevail to make,
What heavy burdens from our bosoms take,
What parched grounds refresh, as with a shower!
We kneel, and all around us seems to lower;
We rise, and all, the distant and the near,
Stands forth in sunny outline, brave and clear;
We kneel how weak, we rise how full of power,
Why therefore should we do ourselves this wrong
Or others—that we are not always strong,
That we are ever overborne with care,
That we should ever weak or heartless be,
Anxious or troubled, when with us in prayer,
And joy and strength and courage are with Thee!

RICHARD CHENEVIX TRENCH, 1807–1886

Love, Worship, Praise, and Adoration
OUR SUNDAY ACTIVITY

"Do You Prepare for Worship?"

Worship: Jesus, You and Me, and Changed Faces

The day Jesus went to worship, His very face was changed. "You're telling me that Jesus went to worship?"

I am. The Bible speaks of a day when Jesus took time to stand with friends in the presence of God to worship: "Jesus took Peter, James, and John up on a high mountain by themselves. While they watched, Jesus' appearance was changed." (Matthew 17:1–2).

> *Christ is not valued at all unless He is valued above all.*
> ST. AUGUSTINE

The simple fact that he chose his companions and went up on the mountain suggests this was no spur-of-the-moment action. Jesus prepared for worship.

Let me ask you, do you do the same? What paths do you take to lead you up the mountain? The question may seem foreign, but my hunch is, many of us simply wake up and show up. We're sadly casual when it comes to meeting God.

Would we be so lackadaisical with, oh, let's say, the president? Suppose you were granted a Sunday morning breakfast at the

White House. How would you spend Saturday night? Would you get ready? Would you collect your thoughts? Of course you would. Should we prepare any less for an encounter with the Holy God?

Let me urge you to come to worship prepared to worship. Pray before you come so you will be ready to pray when you arrive. Sleep before you come so you'll stay alert when you arrive. Read the Word before you come so your heart will be soft when you worship. Come expecting God to speak.

MAX LUCADO
IN *JUST LIKE JESUS*

*Love is the principal, the paramount,
the preeminent, the distinguishing characteristic
of the people of God.
Nothing can dislodge or replace it.
Love is supreme.*
JOHN STOTT IN *THE CONTEMPORARY CHRISTIAN*

The Bond

Array yourselves, then
as God's chosen ones,
His consecrated and dearly loved ones,
in a heart of sympathy,
in kindness, in lowliness,
in gentleness, in tireless patience.

Colossians 3:12 (Way)

The bond that holds God's children together is love, just love.
One unkind deed, one unkind word, one thought even that
moves toward unkindness, is fatal to the quality of love
we must have if His love is to be in us. It is not a little thing
to love like this. Lord, evermore give us this love.

AMY CARMICHAEL
IN *EDGES OF HIS WAYS*

Oh Come, Let Us Sing to the Lord!

*L*et us shout joyfully to the Rock of
    our salvation.
Let us come before His presence
    with thanksgiving;
Let us shout joyfully to Him
    with psalms.
For the LORD is the great God,
And the great King above all gods. . .
Oh come, let us worship
    and bow down;
Let us kneel before the LORD
    our Maker,
For He is our God,
And we are the people of His pasture,
And the sheep of His hand.
Today, if you will hear His voice:
"Do not harden your hearts."

                 Psalm 95:1–3, 6–8, NKJV

The LORD reigns;
Let the earth rejoice;
Let the multitude
*   of isles be glad!*
Rejoice in the LORD,
*   you righteous,*
And give thanks
at the remembrance
*   of His*
*   holy name.*
Psalm 97:1, 12, NKJV

"The Divine Lover"

The reason why the gospel was Good News when it first burst upon the world was simply that men had realized that God is love. The revelation of character provided by Christ Himself showed one thing, that God is by nature Love and that He loves mankind.

It should be obvious that if there is to be a fresh intake of love, it can only come from God Himself, and that it can only be received by those who are willing to be open to God and ready to co-operate with His purpose. For this cleansing and reinvigorating process, we must have deliberate and planned periods of quiet communion with God. Fear will not be driven from our hearts by resolution only, but by the willing reception of the very Spirit of Love. A lot of

this must, I think, be done in private, but a lot more must be done in Christian fellowship. To whatever Church we belong we must meet together to receive in faith the Body and Blood of our Lord. This is our appointment with God, the place and the time where Heaven meets the deficiencies of earth. There can be no doubt that the Young Church renewed, not only its faith and courage, but that deep love which went far beyond the emotions of the fellowship itself by meeting together for "the breaking of bread and the prayers" (Acts 2:42).

J. B. PHILLIPS
IN *NEW TESTAMENT CHRISTIANITY*

Let the beauty of the LORD our God be upon us.
PSALM 90:17, NKJV

He who dwells in the secret place of the Most High shall abide under the shadow of the Almighty. I will say of the LORD, "He is my refuge and my fortress; My God, in Him I will trust."
Psalm 91:1–2, NKJV

David the Psalmist's Great Anthem of Praise

This Psalm was my Mother's favorite Psalm. Widowed in her mid-thirties, left with a ten-year-old son, a five-year-old daughter, and expecting me, she was strong in her faith, devout in teaching us to love the Lord, faithful in training us "in the way we should go," and in keeping Sunday holy. This Psalm, taken from the New King James Version of the Bible, speaks of the psalmist's love of "the house of the LORD," and his confidence in the Lord.

The LORD is my light and my salvation;
Whom shall I fear?
The LORD is the strength of my life;
Of whom shall I be afraid?
One thing I have desired of the LORD, that will I seek;
That I may dwell in the house of the LORD
All the days of my life,
To behold the beauty of the LORD,
And to inquire in His temple,
For in the time of trouble He shall hide me in His pavilion;

In the secret place of His tabernacle He shall hide me;
He shall set me high upon a rock.
I would have lost heart, unless I had believed
That I would see the goodness of the LORD
    in the land of the living.
Wait on the LORD; Be of good courage,
And He shall strengthen your heart;
Wait, I say, on the LORD!

Love Through Me

Love through me, Love of God,
Make me like Thy clear air
Through which, unhindered, colours pass
As though it were not there.

Powers of the love of God,
Depths of the heart Divine,
O Love that faileth not, break forth,
And flood this world of Thine.

AMY CARMICHAEL IN *TOWARD JERUSALEM*

*"For where two
or three are gathered
together in My name,
I am there
in the midst of them."*

Matthew 18:20, NKJV

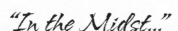

"In the Midst..."

It is not the multitude, but the faith and sincere devotion, of the worshipers, that invites the presence of Christ; and though there be but two or three, the smallest number that can be, yet, if Christ make one among them, who is the principal one, their meeting is as honorable and comfortable as if they were two or three thousand.

MATTHEW HENRY
IN *MATTHEW HENRY'S COMMENTARY VOL. V.*

The Inevitable Christ

The story has come down to us from the early centuries that when the storm of persecution broke over the Christian Church in Rome, the little company of the believers urged Peter to seek refuge in flight. His sense, both of loyalty and of honor, rose up to protest. But his friends pleaded that their deaths would be only the loss of a few sheep of the fold, and his would be the loss of a shepherd. He set out by night along the Appian Way. But as he traveled a vision flashed upon him of a figure clothed in white and a face crowned with thorns. "Quo vadis, domine?" ["Whither goest thou, Lord?"] Peter cried to Christ.

"To Rome, to be crucified instead of Thee."

Into the night the vision ebbed like breath.

And Peter turned and rushed on to Rome and death.

That is a parable of the inevitable Christ. Whether we seek Him or seek Him not, whether we are in the way of our duty or out of it, the vision of Christ shall meet us face to face.

SOURCE UNKNOWN

You Need a Savior

*M*an by himself cannot deal with his own guilt. He must have help from the outside. In order to forgive himself, he must have forgiveness from the one he has offended. Yet man is unworthy to ask God for forgiveness.

That, then, is the whole reason for the cross.

The cross did what man could not do. It granted us the right to talk with, love, and even live with God.

You can't do that by yourself. I don't care how many worship services you attend or good deeds you do, your goodness is insufficient. You can't be good enough to deserve forgiveness. No one bats a thousand. No one bowls 300. No one. Not you, not me, not anyone.

That's why we have guilt in the world.

That's why we need a Savior.

You can't forgive me for my sins nor can I forgive you for yours.

That's why we need a Savior.

Listen. Quit trying to quench your own guilt. You can't do it.

There's no way. Not with a bottle of whiskey or perfect Sunday school attendance. Sorry. I don't care how bad you are. You can't be bad enough to forget it. And I don't care how good you are. You can't be good enough to overcome it.

MAX LUCADO
IN *NO WONDER THEY CALL HIM THE SAVIOR*

Sunday is the golden clasp that binds together the volume of the week.

LONGFELLOW

"For all have sinned and fall short of the glory of God, and are justified freely by his grace through the redemption that came by Christ Jesus."

Romans 3:23–24, NIV

His Sunday Sermons and Senate Prayers

*D*uring the lifetime of Dr. Peter Marshall, and his years in the pulpit of Washington's historic New York Avenue Presbyterian Church and as Chaplain of the United States Senate, people stood in line for hours each Sunday surrounding the church, waiting to hear him preach. Senators left their committee meetings to listen to his famous Senate prayers. A selection of these sermons and prayers were made into a best-selling book *Mr. Jones, Meet the Master*. Here is one of those memorable prayers:

Our Father, we are beginning to understand
at last that the things that are wrong with our
world are the sum total of all the things that are wrong
with us as individuals. Thou hast made us after Thine
image, and our hearts can find no rest until they rest in Thee.
We are too Christian really to enjoy sinning and too fond of sinning to
enjoy Christianity. Most of us know perfectly well what we ought to
do; our trouble is that we do not want to do it. Thy help is our only
hope. Make us want to do what is right, and give us the ability to do
it. In the name of Christ our Lord. AMEN.

"Carriers" of Christ

*M*en are mirrors, or "carriers" of Christ to other men. Sometimes unconscious carriers. This "good infection" can be carried by those who have not got it themselves. People who were not Christians themselves helped me to Christianity. But usually it is those who know Him that bring Him to others. That is why the Church, the whole body of Christians showing Him to one another, is so important. You might say that when two Christians are following Christ together there is not twice as much Christianity as when they are apart, but sixteen times as much.

Christians are Christ's body, the organism through which He works. Every addition to that body enables Him to do more. If you want to help those outside you must add your own little cell to the body of Christ who alone can help them.

C. S. LEWIS
IN *MERE CHRISTIANITY*

Like a River Glorious

Text by Frances Ridley Havergal

The words of this beautiful hymn are among my own personal favorites. Read these lyrics and let the truth of these words wash over you with the peace that only God can provide: "You will keep him in perfect peace, whose mind is stayed on You, because he trusts in You. Trust in the LORD forever, for in Yah, the LORD, is everlasting strength." Isaiah 26:3–4, NKJV

Like a river glorious
is God's perfect peace.
Over all victorious
in its bright increase;
Perfect, yet it floweth
fuller every day,
Perfect, yet it groweth
deeper all the way.

Hidden in the hollow
of His blessed hand,
Never foe can follow,
Never traitor stand;
Not a surge of worry,
Not a shade of care,
Not a blast of hurry
Touch the spirit there.

Every joy or trial
Falleth from above,
Traced upon our dial
By the Sun of Love.
We may trust Him fully
All for us to do;
They who trust Him wholly
Find Him wholly true.

Stayed upon Jehovah, hearts are fully blest;
Finding, as He promised, perfect peace and rest.

Faith and Devotion

OBSERVING SUNDAY

The Immortal Dreamer

The Tinker of Bedford—The Man Who Spent Twelve Years in Prison Because He Remained Faithful to His Calling

$\mathcal{J}$ohn Bunyan, best known for the immortal work, *The Pilgrim's Progress,* died August 31, 1688. At his funeral in Whitechapel, London, George Cokayan said, "It is remarkably strange that this man who came into the world under such poor circumstances and lived a portion of his life under the most handicapped conditions did such a great work. Nearly twelve years he spent in Bedford Jail as a religious prisoner, suffering for the freedom he craved. He lived almost sixty years and leaves behind him exactly sixty books—a book for every year of his life.

"The candle which John Bunyan has lighted in England shall never be put out. Above all his other works, *The Pilgrim's Progress* already has gone far enough over many lands to see that it may become one of England's greatest contributions to the literature of this century."

Certainly, he was an unusual and God-ordained man. With little formal education, he wrote books and, with no formal legal training, helped secure religious freedom in English law. Most of this was accomplished in prison. He profoundly influenced his countrymen through the power of his pen, which no prison walls could still. He was jailed repeatedly for preaching without a license. Through it all, John Bunyan remained faithful to his calling as he saw it. His dedication to Jesus Christ and fervor for the gospel were acknowledged finally even by his enemies. His vision endures in one of the consistently best-selling books, *The Pilgrim's Progress*. His love for Sunday, and the opportunity it afforded to preach the Word, are legendary in Christian history.

SELECTED AND RETOLD

"This is Christ, who continually with the Oil of His Grace maintains the work already begun in the heart: By the means of which…the souls of His people prove gracious still."

JOHN BUNYAN
IN *THE PILGRIM'S PROGRESS*

He that would prepare for heaven must honor the Sabbath upon earth.
D. WILSON

The Jailer
Who Sought Salvation at a Sunday Service

*P*rovidentially, even though in jail, very often John Bunyan was able to preach to his jail brethren and to believers who gathered at the jail for Sunday services. On one such occasion, late in January, 1665, he searched his soul and the Word for a suitable text. His mind was led to St. Paul's words, "This is a faithful saying, and worthy of all acceptation, that Christ Jesus came into the world to save sinners; of whom I am chief" (1 Timothy 1:15, KJV).

The morning air was filled with expectancy. People stood outside the jail to hear their much-loved and respected friend and neighbor. Paul Cobb, jailer, opened the huge jail door so that John could stand in the doorway and preach both to those on the inside and those on the outside. John stood in the doorway, opened his Bible, and read the text. "Today, dear friends, I am going to preach to you upon the subject, 'Grace Abounding to the Chief of Sinners.'"

Despite himself, the jailer listened as John Bunyan gave his own testimony. "I was once the chief of sinners, too, roaming these hills and fields, swearing and drinking and lying and stealing. I was a no-good rascal, condemned to die forever."

The jailer was stricken by a mighty sense of his own sin. He bowed his head, tears came to his eyes. When John finished his sermon, he spoke up. "John, may I say a word? I stand today a convicted sinner. John Bunyan's life has shown me as nothing else ever has that his religion is true and able to do for him what religion ought to do for a man. Today, I believe God for Christ's sake has forgiven and redeemed my soul. I feel this sermon was just for my soul."

SELECTED AND RETOLD

"Christ Jesus came into the world to save sinners—of whom I am the worst. But for that very reason I was shown mercy so that in me, the worst of sinners, Christ Jesus might display his unlimited patience as an example for those who would believe on him and receive eternal life."

1 Timothy 1:15–16, NIV

Presidents
and the Observance of the Lord's Day

* *G*eorge Washington in the Revolutionary War, Lincoln in the Civil War, and Wilson in World War I all gave orders relieving troops as far as possible from fatigue duty on Sunday, and giving them opportunity to attend public worship.

* *H*ayes and Garfield
habitually walked to church
that their servants might rest
and worship on the Lord's Day.

* *G*rant, when at Paris, refused to attend horse races on the Lord's Day.

* *M*cKinley, when at the opening of the State Centennial of Tennessee, refused a trip up Lookout Mountain saying, "No, I do not go sightseeing on Sunday."

* *T*heodore Roosevelt and Coolidge spoke in appreciation of the Lord's Day; the latter said, "I profoundly believe in the Lord's Day."

* *I*t was a fixed habit of Theodore Roosevelt to attend church on Sunday and he continued it all his years in Washington. The pastor of his church always received a letter or phone message from the president when he expected to be out of town, explaining his absence.

* *P*resident Truman, fishing on the Columbia River, refused to cast a line on Sunday.

* *O*n Sunday morning, September 27, 1959, President Eisenhower invited Khrushchev to accompany him to a worship service at Gettysburg Presbyterian Church. The Communist leader declined and Eisenhower went without him.

President Carter was highly respected for his Christian conduct and devotion to worship on Sunday.

The Olympic Runner Who Stood Firm

*F*or months Eric Liddell trained with the hope of winning the 100-meter race at the Olympic races of 1924. Many sportswriters predicted he would win. Then Eric learned the 100-meter race was scheduled for Sunday. This posed a problem: Eric believed that he could not honor God by running in the contest on the Lord's Day. His fans were stunned by his refusal. Some who had praised him now called him a fool. But Eric stood firm.

Suddenly a runner dropped out of the 400-meter race, scheduled on a weekday. Eric offered to fill the slot, even though this was four times as long as the race for which he had trained.

When the race was run, Eric Liddell set a record of 47.6 seconds—the winner.

Later, Eric Liddell went to China as a missionary. He died there in 1945, in a prisoner of war camp.

Contemplative Thought
in a Chapel on Sunday

The great psychologist, William James, told us that the practice of going to a quiet place which was suggestive of contemplative thought aided in keeping one's point of view right side up. He said that going to chapel was much like the experience of a person who, being jostled about in a crowd, climbs up on a nearby doorstep, looks over the heads of the people, sees what the crowd as a whole is doing, and is then able to descend again into the jam and push in the right direction.

AUSTEN FOX RIGGS, M.D.

Lord, Begin with Me!

The evangelist Gypsy Smith was asked one day, "What can I do so that a revival will take place in my church?"

The answer was, "Go into your room and take a piece of chalk; draw a circle on the floor and kneel down in the middle of it. Then pray: 'Lord, bring revival to my church, and begin in the middle of this circle.'"

SOURCE UNKNOWN

Sunday School
and the Call of God

> *"It seems God must have been calling me from the first day I knew about good and bad."*

$\mathscr{D}$r. John R. Rice was one of the great evangelists of the twentieth century. He was known as "America's dean of evangelists." He told about the influence of Sunday school on his young life:

"At about four, I was taught in Sunday school about the baby Jesus and how He had to be born in an old stable because they had no room for Him in the inn. I kept that little picture Sunday school card given me that day and felt guilty in my own heart that people like me had no room for Jesus.

"When I was about five I was deeply moved by a song my mother sang, 'Turned Away from the Beautiful Gate.' Even then I seemed to know that it was by their own sinful rebellion and rejection of Christ that people missed heaven. I remember my unrest of soul.

"When Mother lay on her deathbed she talked of the Savior

and had all of us promise to meet her in heaven. I felt myself under the spell of her dying smile and testimony until I trusted Christ.

"After Mother's death, I remembered the tears and exhortations of my Sunday school teacher; the godly pastor telling the story of the prodigal son and how he had run away from home and came to want and trouble, and how he was forgiven upon his return.

"It seems God must have been calling me from the first day I knew about good and bad."

COMPILED BY PETER F. GUNTHER
FROM *GREAT SERMONS OF THE 20TH CENTURY*

*"Who may live
on your holy hill?
He whose walk
is blameless
and who does
what is righteous,
who speaks the truth
from his heart
and has no slander
on his tongue."*
Psalm 15:1–3, NIV

I Am His
and He Is Mine!

Eugenia Price lived, in her own words, "in the world of paganism for almost eighteen years." This devotional is from her book, Discoveries Made from Living My New Life.

I am His and He is mine! That is my theology. It is very simple and I have discovered to my great and eternal joy that it works.

I did not become a Christian to save myself from eternal damnation. I did not become a Christian to make certain my passage to heaven. I did not think about either hell or heaven when I was being moved within by the Holy Spirit of Jesus Christ. I was captivated by the One who holds "captivity captive"!

I did not pick and choose among the various churches during the time the Holy Spirit bore down upon my brittle heart. I did not think much one way or another about churches. I had not been inside one in almost eighteen years and although I love them now and believe every new Christian must unite his life and efforts with some Christian group, at that moment when the Holy Spirit pressed in upon my sin-encrusted con-sciousness, I did not think of churches. I thought about Christ! And the more I thought about Him, the more real He became to me; and the more real He became, the more I wanted Him to be mine. And then my simple the-ology came into being. He seemed to say: "I'll be yours if you'll be mine."

My discoveries about the Christian life can be included in one sweeping overall discovery: I belong to Him and He belongs to me! In the person of the Holy Spirit, my Lord is with me and in me as I work and play and laugh and weep and love on the earth. I am one of His sheep. I know His name.

To my great, glad amazement, I have discovered that I am His and He is mine–forever!

> *"Oh, this full and perfect peace! Oh, this transport all divine! In a love which cannot cease, I am His and He is mine."*
> GEORGE W. ROBINSON

Gladstone Turns Down Pompeii

*W*hen Gladstone visited Naples, the authorities, wishing to show him special honor, arranged an excursion to visit Pompeii, and, without consulting him, chose Sunday for the trip. The papers announced that Gladstone and his party would go by special steamer on Sunday to an excavation at Pompeii, and this was telegraphed to all countries. But when the hour came this truly great man was found in his regular place with the people of God, and he did not visit Pompeii until Tuesday.

> *"I owe my life and vigor, through a long and busy life, to the Sabbath day, with its blessed surcease of toil."*
>
> W. E. GLADSTONE

It was Gladstone who said: "Tell me what the young men of England are doing on Sunday, and I will tell you what the future of England will be."

He is also remembered for saying, "All that I think, all that I hope, all that I write, all that I live for, is based upon the divinity of Jesus Christ, the central joy of my poor, wayward life."

How Dwight L. Moody Was Saved

On April 21, 1855, a Sunday school teacher stood in front of a Boston shoe store, indecision written on his face. He wanted to visit a young member of his class who was a clerk in the store, but he did not want to embarrass the boy in front of his friends. He hesitated, walked past, then determined to make a dash for it and have it over at once.

He found the boy in the back wrapping shoes in paper and putting them on shelves. He went up to him and put his hand on his shoulder, and simply told him of Christ's love and the love Christ wanted in return.

The young man received Christ as his Savior right there in the storeroom of the shoe store. He made application to join a local congregation but was turned down because of his spiritual ignorance. A year later he applied again and was received—though with some reluctance. His name: Dwight L. Moody.

When the Royal Box Was Empty

On a visit to Venice, that city prepared an elaborate performance at one of the principal theaters for Emperor William of Germany. The performance was set for a Sunday evening. When the Emperor was informed of what had been done and was asked to honor the assembly with his presence, he replied, "Since I have become Emperor I have made it a principle of my life never to attend any place of amusement on the Lord's Day."

King Humbert followed the Emperor's example. As both Emperor and King were expected, the theater was crowded from floor to ceiling, but the royal box was empty. The brilliant gathering learned a lesson on the duty of keeping holy the Lord's Day.

Let us value our Christian heritage, including the day of rest and gladness, which far too often we take for granted.

$\mathcal{T}$herefore we also, since we are surrounded by so great a cloud of witnesses, let us lay aside every weight, and the sin which so easily ensnares us, and let us run with endurance the race that is set before us, looking unto Jesus, the author and finisher of our faith, who for the joy that was set before Him endured the cross, despising the shame, and has sat down at the right hand of the throne of God.

For consider Him who endured such hostility from sinners against Himself, lest you become weary and discouraged in your souls. You have not yet resisted to bloodshed, striving against sin. . . .

But you have come to Mount Zion and to the city of the living God, the heavenly Jerusalem, to an innumerable company of angels, to the general assembly and church of the firstborn who are registered in heaven, to God the Judge of all, to the spirits of just men made perfect, to Jesus the Mediator of the new covenant, and to the blood of sprinkling.

HEBREWS 12:1–4, 22–24, NKJV

1. BEETHOVEN: Pastoral Symphony, 2nd Movement (11:41) (Scene by the Brook) *Performed by The Hanover Band, directed by Roy Goodman and Monica Huggett*
2. MOZART: Clarinet Concerto in 'A' K622, 2nd Movement (07:14) *Performed by The Hanover Band, directed by Roy Goodman with Colin Lawson, basset clarinet*

3. BEETHOVEN: Pastoral Symphony, 1st Movement (10:45) (Awakening of happy feelings on arrival in the country)*Performed by The Hanover Band, directed by Roy Goodman and Monica Huggett*
4. MOZART: Clarinet Concerto in 'A' K622, 1st Movement (12:45) *Performed by The Hanover Band, directed by Roy Goodman with Colin Lawson, basset clarinet*
5. BEETHOVEN: Pastoral Symphony, Last Movement (09:11) (Happy and thank full feelings after the storm)*Performed by The Hanover Band, directed by Roy Goodman and Monica Huggett*
6. MOZART: Clarinet Concerto in 'A' K622, 3rd Movement (08:44) *Performed by The Hanover Band, directed by Roy Goodman with Colin Lawson, basset clarinet*

TOTAL RUNNING TIME (60:20)

Sunday

Sunda

nday Sun

Sunday

Sunday
Sunday
Sunday
nday Sun
Sunday